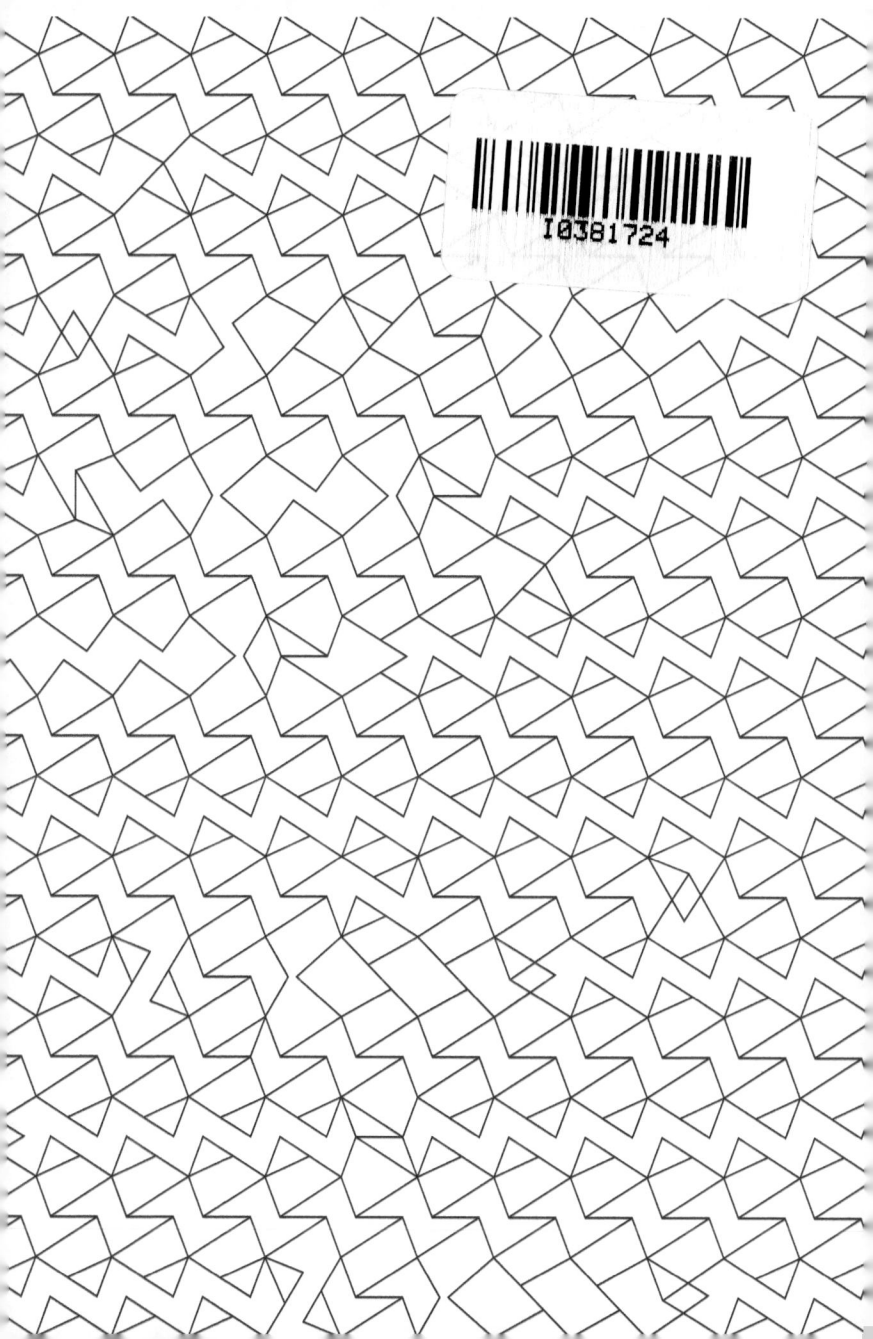

Obscure & Irregular

Stories by Eli S. Evans

" ......
....
...... "

Moon Rabbit Books & Ephemera

Lawrence, Kansas

2021

First published in 2021 by

The Moon Rabbit Books & Ephemera Corporation

a wholly-owned subsidiary of

The Moon Rabbit Drinking Club & Benevolence Society
(a now-defunct not-for-profit literary conglomerate)

www.moonrabbitbooks.com

PO Box # 3 / Lawrence, Kansas 66044 / U.S.A.

Copyright © Eli S. Evans, 2021

All rights reserved

*The right of Eli S. Evans to be identified as the author of this work
has been asserted by him in accordance with
the Copyright, Designs, and Patents Act of 1988.*

Library of Congress Control Number: 2020923509
ISBN 978-1-7348930-0-7 (print); 978-1-7348930-1-4 (ebook)

Illustrated by
Patrick Giroux

Designed by
Patrick Giroux and Jay Holley

Read by
Celebrities and literary powerhouses, mostly

21 20 19 18 17 16 15 14 12 11 10 9 8 7 6 5 4 3 2 1

First Edition

This is a work of fiction. All characters, coffee shops, and events
portrayed in these stories are products of the author's imagination
and are used fictitiously.

For the idea of plot, for graciously leaving me in peace...

Stories

Care & Feeding	Rastafarian Banana, *p. 8*
	A Passing Thought, *p. 12*
Social Relations	New With Stu, *p. 14*
	The Old Friend, *p. 18*
Modern Medicine	A Minor Procedure, *p. 22*
	Wart, Two Ways, *p. 39*
Street Culture	Street, Two Ways, *p. 42*
	A Shot On the Calle Murguía, *p. 43*
Distracted Driving	On the Kindness of Others, *p. 48*
	Too Much Too Soon, *p. 50*

Rastafarian Banana

I was driving from the small town in which I currently reside to another, bigger town about a half hour away, to have coffee with a friend who happened to be "in town," in the generic sense of being in the general vicinity (in fact, she was staying in a town that was neither the town in which I currently reside nor the town in which we would be meeting for coffee). I looked forward to seeing my friend, who I hadn't seen since the last time we'd seen each other, but not so much to possibly seeing her husband, who was definitely in town with her and therefore could conceivably have been planning to join in the coffee meet-up (I hadn't asked directly, to avoid creating the wrong impression). The reason I was not looking forward to seeing him was

that he, like me, is a writer, but as a result of some recent good fortune had, by virtually any applicable metric, now become a more successful one—for instance, he'd had a book (of poetry, albeit) accepted for publication by a well-regarded press, and would in the fall assume a more prestigious university post than mine, at a more prestigious university. In short, I didn't want to see him not because I disliked him or

found him unpleasant, but because doing so would mean facing up to his accomplishments and, by comparison, my own lack thereof (for instance, I did not have a book coming out, nor as prestigious a university post at as prestigious a university), and facing up to my own lack of accomplishments was something I very much did (and still do) dislike and find unpleasant. To prepare for the possible encounter and the emotions I anticipated it provoking—or, I suppose, to cope with the emotions I was for all intents and purposes experiencing in advance, in my very anticipation of experiencing them—I'd taken an extra dose of the anti-anxiety medication a dose of which I take every morning before or after I brush my teeth; as usual, it hadn't had much of an effect.

It was a very hot day here in the interior of New England, where all of the towns in question are located, and the air was so thick that when I'd tried to take my aging dog for his morning walk, I'd been forced to reverse course after just a few minutes because he appeared to be suffocating. That was around seven, when the sun was still low in the sky; now, as I turned left onto a road that would take me through a town, heretofore unmentioned, on the far side of which I would turn left again onto the road that would take me all the way into the town to which I was *en route* for coffee, the temperatures had climbed into the mid-nineties and a bright white sun hung high in the cloudless sky. A certain song came on the radio that I felt might help prepare me, where the medication had failed, for this possible encounter with my friend's husband and by way of it with myself, and I turned the volume up in order that more of the song might enter me, or the same amount might enter me more intensely, and that was when I passed, on my right, a rather unexpected sight: curbside in front of an old farmstead-style house, not architecturally atypical of the region, someone had deposited a large stuffed banana (I would estimate that it measured roughly four feet from end to end) with a piece of paper taped to it on which the word FREE had been scrawled in bold capital letters. The banana was partially anthropomorphized in the fashion of an aggressively stereotyped Rastafarian, with big, bloodshot eyes, imitation black dreadlocks hanging from the edges of its hat (a crocheted beanie of the sort in which the iconic reggae musician Bob Marley was so often photographed), and what was meant to be a large marijuana cigarette dangling from a mouth opened into a wide, toothy grin. Meanwhile, a woman—her own car parked at an

angle that indicated it had been pulled off the road hastily, with the driver's side door left slightly ajar as though, once parked, she had no less hastily made her exit from it—was evidently trying to decide whether or not she should take the banana, regarding it, as one might a pair of factory seconds socks at a discount department store, first from nearer and then from farther, first from this angle and then from that, before finally picking it up and giving it a little squeeze and a shake as though to test its density or weight.

As I drove on, past the post office and, after that, through the center of town, where the two-lane road's two lanes split to circumvent a small triangle of grass atop which local musicians give free concerts on certain summer evenings, what I thought was that, finding himself in a similar situation, my friend's husband perhaps would not suffer from a similar failure of imagination, and that perhaps this, more than good fortune,  was why he had become a more successful writer than me—but that for my part, I simply could not fathom what mysterious calculations this woman might have been making, standing there by the side of the road beneath a blaring midday summer sun trying to decide whether or not to take the gigantic stuffed Rastafarian banana somebody else was just trying to give away.

A Passing Thought

Cresting a rise and coming around a bend on a country road on the way to a summer arts and performance festival popular with cosmopolitan-minded residents of various urban and exurban population centers both near and not quite as near, I pass, on my right, the entrance to "Bannish Lumber." It occurs to me that if your last name is Bannish, it might be best not to partake of the in any event somewhat antiquated tradition of bestowing it upon the family business—or, if you are committed to doing so, to at the very least append to it an "& sons" or "& co."[1] This strikes me as a thought worth sharing, but because my son (who at his current age wouldn't know what I was talking about, anyway) is asleep in the backseat and my wife (who for her part is already plenty familiar with my schtick) has insisted on silence in order to safeguard his slumber, instead of sharing it with them I compose a little story about it in my mind as a way of sharing it with that imaginary audience to whom every act of literary speech is directed. *Cresting a rise and coming around a bend on a country road*, the story begins—and by now, you can probably guess the end.

---

1 Upon further consideration, I have determined that this guideline in fact applies only if the second part of the name of your business describes or identifies the specific goods or services or category of goods or services in which your business traffics, or identifies your business as or with a specific place or category of place, but in the plural, such as in the case of a business with multiple locations. However, if the second part of the name of your business identifies your business as or with a specific place or category of place in the singular, Bannish works perfectly well.† To put it more concretely: while the name Bannish Lumberyards (imagining a Bannish family that owns multiple lumberyards) would be problematic in the same way, and for the same reasons, as the name Bannish Lumber, the name Bannish Lumberyard, in the singular (and presuming, in this case, a Bannish family that owns only a single lumberyard), would not.

† In theory, the last name Bannish would not present any problems if the second part of the name of the business in question did not identify either the goods or services (specifically or categorically) in which said business trafficked, or identify said business with a place (again, specific or categorical), but it is difficult, if not impossible, to imagine what such a name might look like. On the other hand, alone in its possessive form, the last name Bannish works as well as any other as the name of a business, which in this case would be called Bannish's, and would probably be a restaurant, café, tavern, or inn.◊

◊ If one were in the business of bannisters, whether their production, distribution, installation, or some combination of the foregoing, fusing surname and category of good and/or service offered by way of the obvious pun—Bannish-ters (without or with out the hyphen)—would render void all of the above considerations, and probably various others, as well.

New with Stu

Almost by chance, during a conversation with a friend of mine who is also friends with him, I asked what was new with Stu, who I myself would consider less a friend than an acquaintance or, this arguably denoting a slightly more elevated status, a close friend of close friends who I do not know especially well but assume, because of the close friendships by which our acquaintanceship is mediated, would have been worthy of closer friendship had our respective personalities and lifestyle preferences (for instance, he abstained from drugs and alcohol as a rule, whereas I abstained from drugs only out of a combination of trepidation and habit, and did not abstain from alcohol at all) been more compatible when our lives overlapped during a summertime residency for people working in or adjacent to a particular field of study at a university in the western part of a state in the eastern part of the United States several years ago.

As it turned out, since I'd last received news of him, Stu had left his job teaching at a boarding school in the Midwest, moved to New York City to pursue a career in stand-up comedy, abandoned his career in stand-up comedy, gone to South America with his life savings in his pocket, traveled vagabond-style for many months, hiking and hitchhiking and hopping onto train cars, sleeping on the floors of strangers' shacks or outside under stars or rain, sipping from unmarked bottles of alcohol or draw-

ing from pipes packed with unspecified substances of unknown provenance as they were passed around this or that circle of fellow travelers he'd only just met, until eventually, somewhere in the Peruvian Amazon, he decided, if indeed he was still in a condition to make what could properly be characterized as a decision, to place himself in the hands of the shaman who oversaw him during the ten days he spent in a cave "tripping balls," as the saying goes, on the hallucinogen ayahuasca (an ancient drug described in a recent report in the *New Yorker* magazine as "the latest trend in Brooklyn and Silicon Valley"), from which experience (and cave) he emerged convinced that, despite having identified as heterosexual for as long as he was capable of making such an identification, he was actually homosexual. After that, Stu gave up drugs and other mind-altering substances such as alcohol, concluding that he'd gotten everything he could out of them, determined that his trip to South America had reached its natural terminus for much the same reason, returned to New York City and his floundering career as a stand-up comic, and came out as a proud gay man via a lengthy narrative screed distributed across various social media. In response to that announcement, he received a predictable outpouring of support from many of the friends and acquaintances with whom he'd remained connected over the years by way of those same social media but suffered a brief estrangement from his simultaneously politically progressive and culturally conservative nuclear family. They reconciled soon enough, but not before, out of money and unable to ask them for help due to the estrangement, he'd found himself compelled to apply for, and when it was offered accept, a job teaching at a boarding school in the Midwest. Only a few weeks after beginning this new job, he met a woman to whom, after only a few months of dating, he became engaged to be married, and since he had announced that engagement in a post distributed across, once again, the very same social media, only a few weeks earlier, I could now consider myself, my friend informed me, pretty much up to date as far as Stu was concerned.

My first thought, upon hearing all of this, was that as it could not have been more than two years since I'd last received news of Stu, it was unreasonable for so many things of such great magnitude to be new with him. But then I realized that in so far as the last I knew of him, he was a heterosexual man who abstained from drugs and alcohol and worked as a teacher at a boarding school in the Midwest, from my own personal perspective the only thing that was actually new with him was that he had become engaged, something that, all things considered, did not seem so unreasonable at all.

The Old Friend

He is such an old friend, and I have moved about so much in recent years, that he does not even know where I am currently living. Still, when he posts, to a photo-sharing service to which we both subscribe, a picture of himself from just a few miles away, I send him an enthusiastic message by way of the same service informing him that he is in, as it were, my "neck of the woods." It turns out that his girlfriend as of the previous spring (prior to that he must have had a different girlfriend, unless the person in those pictures was his sister) is living in a nearby town while she oversees the construction of a new building at a university in another nearby town, and he will be visiting until the following Sunday. We concur that we should, that we *must*, get together while he is here. Tonight is no good for either of us, and tomorrow as well presents certain problems, but we will, we agree, be in touch later in the week to work something out.

On Wednesday morning I send him a message offering to drive to the nearby town in which his girlfriend is living to meet him for an afternoon coffee or beer, depending on his preference, but he indicates that today it will not be possible as he plans to accompany his girlfriend to another town where she will have the tires (having been raised in a British colony, he describes them as "tyres") changed on her car. Coincidentally, the town to which he will be accompanying his girlfriend is even nearer to the town in which I am currently residing than the town in which his girlfriend is currently residing, and is

moreover home to an excellent bar, where I would be happy to meet him for an afternoon beer, and an acceptable coffee shop where, if he is not up for an afternoon beer (we grow old, we grow old), I would be happy to meet him for an afternoon coffee. After informing him of this, I do not hear from him for several hours, then at last receive a message informing me that he unfortunately did not receive my message until after he and his girlfriend had already left the town in which her tires ("tyres") had been changed.

As it is still August, and I am employed on an academic

schedule, I have plenty of free time, so I write back offering to drive that evening to the town in which his girlfriend is currently residing to meet him for a beer or even—since evening would be too late for coffee—a tea, which I hate but would nonetheless be willing to drink for the pleasure of seeing him. If tonight doesn't work, however, I tell him that I could also drive in tomorrow, Thursday, to meet up for a morning coffee, an afternoon  beer or coffee, or an evening beer or tea, and would be equally able to do so at any of the same times, and for any of the same beverages, on Friday, to which information I add that it should go without saying that he, alone or with his girlfriend, is welcome, at whatever hour suits him or them best, to come to my house today, tomorrow, or Friday, where he would have the opportunity to meet my child, who had not yet been conceived the last time he and I saw each other, and greet my wife, who thinks of him in only the fondest terms.

Again, I do not hear from him for a period of several hours, at the conclusion of which I receive the following message: "I'll double-check with the girlfriend, but I'm pretty sure I'm going to be busy that day." I am only saved from the pain of having been blown off by an old friend by the fact that he is now an ex-friend.

A Minor Procedure

I'm 41 years old, but I had to go in for my first colonoscopy—which in normal cases one is permitted to delay until the age of 50—as a result of the fact that I've had a stomachache since October (it's late March, as I write these words), and after talking to me for approximately five to seven minutes and pressing lightly on my abdomen for approximately two to three, Dr. Patel, the gastroenterologist I'd waited two months to see after at last managing to wrangle a referral from my primary care provider, who seems to have never met a symptom she didn't think was probably nothing, determined that he could make no diagnosis, and accordingly formulate no plan for treatment, without first performing a colonoscopy. "Don't worry," he said. "It's just a minor procedure."

The preparations for the colonoscopy were completely terrible, which isn't to say that anything went wrong during them, but only that the preparations for a colonoscopy, even when they go entirely as intended, are completely terrible. What follows are the instructions, exactly as I typed them out while talking to a woman who called me on behalf of Dr. Patel approximately a week before the procedure:

- Five days before: Do not eat raw fruit, raw vegetables, corn, beets, granola, nuts, seeds, red food dye, purple food dye. If you take warfarin (?), stop taking warfarin (do I take warfarin?).
- Pick up prep from Walgreens. Refrigerate so it doesn't taste as bad.
- Sunday: Light breakfast Sunday morning (white toast, boiled or poached eggs—not scrambled—no bread with seeds or nuts). After 9AM, nothing besides clear liquids—Jello (not red or purple), popsicles (not real fruit popsicles, not red or purple), water, coffee (no milk or creamer), sports beverages (not red or purple), chicken broth.
- Between 4-6 o' clock, start prep. Drink first dose, following instructions, and then more clear liquids are permitted.
- Monday: Start second dose of prep at 9:30AM *latest*. After 10:30, nothing nothing nothing. Arrive at hospital by 1:30PM. Procedure will not be performed unless a responsible adult is on hand to drive me home afterwards. May not travel by bus or taxi.

As a young Jew with occasionally spiritual pretensions, I fasted various times for Yom Kippur, the Jewish Day of Atonement, so the not eating for upwards of thirty hours part of the preparation was no big problem. Less so the so-called "prep," as the woman on the phone must have described it, since that's how I wrote it down. This prep—a "preparation" in the more technical sense of the word, that is to say, a substance created for medical purposes from a mixture of other substances—is an exceedingly powerful laxative the purpose of which is to drain your colon in order that when the doctor looks at it through a small camera inserted into your anus, this being the essence of the colonoscopy, his (in this case, his) view not be obstructed by the load of feces that is normally wadded up inside there like a clog in a drain.

Not long after drinking the first dose of prep, as promised by the literature on the back of the packaging in which it had been delivered to me by a pharmacist with an apologetic expression on her face, I experienced an urgent need to have a bowel movement, but (also as also promised by the literature on the back of the packaging) what happened when I sat down on the toilet to relieve that urge was not a bowel movement as I had ever known one prior. Instead, it was a mighty spray of liquified fecal matter, a firehose blast that, when it hit the toilet water, produced the sound of a horse or elephant urinating. This went on for several hours, one such episode followed so closely by the next that it didn't seem worth the effort to get off the toilet between them; meanwhile my wife and child went on enjoying their lives, or at least that was how it sounded from where I was sitting, in a distant sector of the house. At last, when I felt like there was nothing left inside me, I went to sleep, and slept well, though a bit hungrily, only to be awakened at quarter to six the next morning to discover there was something left inside me, after all.

Around 7:30, when I was feeling really and truly emptied out, my wife left to take our child to school and herself to work, and I took my dog for a short walk, during which—perhaps out of sympathy for my circumstances—he did not defecate, as is his normal custom at that time of day. After that, I was left with about an hour and a half to kill before the time came to start my second dose of the prep, and so I sat on my bed with my computer and my guitar, which I play very poorly, and watched some videos that were meant to teach me how to play it better. This part of the preparation probably doesn't sound so bad, but there was something desolate about it, as though the void the prep had opened up inside of me had in turn opened onto a void of a different sort, and now there was nothing to do but contemplate it. I considered making a video of myself playing the guitar—something I had never done and, if I did, would surely never show to anyone—but was discouraged by the presence, for nearly a week by that point, of two enormous pimples on my forehead, side-by-side like a pair of fraternal twins enduring a difficult stage of life. By the time I'd made up my mind, on account of the pimples, to definitely not make this video that I would definitely never show to anyone, it was time for the second dose.

This second dose caused me to once again experience an urgent need to have a bowel movement, but when I sat on the toilet nothing noteworthy came of it. Nonetheless, I stayed there for well over an hour. During most of this time, I was playing a word game on the telephone. At first, I made moves in the games I currently had going with my mother and two friends, but since none of them played back—probably because they were doing things other than sitting on a toilet playing the word game—I decided to do something I'd never done before, which was participate in a "Lightning Round." The Lightning Round entailed teaming up (we were the "Blue Team") with five other random people out there in the world who had joined a Lightning Round at about the same moment I had, and competing against another group of six random people (the "Purple Team") who had done the same. Several boards were active simultaneously, although one could only play one of them at a time, and the objective was to collectively reach 750 total points before the other team. Once the game was over, a screen showed who on your team had scored how many points. This was informative but also agitating, because over the course of various Lightning Rounds, whenever my team lost, I would turn out to have been the highest scorer, and whenever my team won someone else would turn out to have been the highest scorer. When at last my team won *and* I was its highest scorer, which was the result I'd been striving for, I did not feel the sense of accomplishment my striving had foretold. Instead, I realized I'd been on the toilet so long my legs had gone numb and felt a great sense of regret for the time I'd wasted sitting there playing a word game on my phone, notwithstanding the fact that all I'd been doing prior to that was wasting time in other ways (although an argument could certainly be made that time wasted playing the guitar is less wasted than time wasted sitting on the toilet trying to achieve a particular result in a word game on your phone, no matter how poorly you play the guitar or how well the word game). Then again, I may have stayed on the toilet so long because completion of the second dose of prep and ensuing bowel movement was, as it were, the last station stop between me and my final destination, which was the colonoscopy itself, and subconsciously I might have been trying to delay confronting—psychically, I mean—the colonoscopy itself.

To be clear, I was not afraid of the actual colonoscopy. Yes, according to Dr. Patel, a four-foot tube would be inserted into my colon by way of my anus, and no, I had never had something of comparable dimensions inserted into my colon or any other part of my body by way of my anus. However, I wasn't going to actually experience having this four-foot tube inserted into my colon by way of my anus because I was going to be sedated with Propofol, a drug that, though not technically a general anesthetic because one continues to breathe on his (in this case, his) own under its influence, renders one completely and irreparably unconscious until shortly after it ceases to be delivered to the bloodstream.

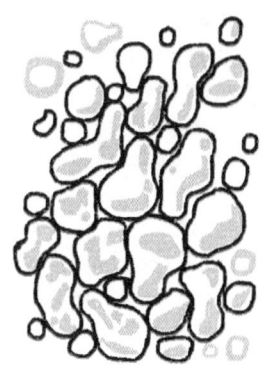

Unfortunately, I was afraid of the Propofol. For one thing, it was the drug that had killed the pop star Michael Jackson. Dr. Patel assured me, when I pointed this out to him, that the reason Propofol killed Michael Jackson was first of all that Michael Jackson had taken way too much of it, and second of all that he was not being actively monitored while under its effects, while I would be both given an appropriate dose of it and closely monitored by an actual anesthesiologist before, during, and after it was administered. I mentioned that I'd read somewhere that because for months before his death, Jackson had experienced only Propofol-induced sleep, which doesn't include the Rapid Eye Movement, or REM, stage, which is the part of sleep that really counts as sleep, some people say that if the Propofol hadn't killed him, he likely would have soon died of sleep deprivation instead. Dr. Patel looked at me with skeptical irritation, like I was that annoying kind of person who talks with confidence about things he knows nothing about to people who know a lot about those very things, but I did not find this attitude reasonable, since I was not asserting that what I'd said about Michael Jackson was true but only that I'd read that some people had said it was true. Anyway, even with Dr. Patel's assurances and reassurances I found the prospect of being rendered unconscious by the Propofol frightening insofar as being unconscious necessarily entails the possibility of never regaining consciousness. In that case, one of course might point out, I should have been wary of going to sleep at night, but if I didn't sleep at night, I could die of sleep deprivation the way some people, according to what I'd read on the internet, said Michael Jackson would have if he hadn't overdosed on Propofol first. Well, that's more or less where I was at in my thinking when my wife came home, having ended her workday early in order to have enough time to eat lunch and walk the dog before driving me to the hospital for my procedure. While she prepared herself lunch, she talked to me at length about a colleague who after performing a certain set of tasks surprisingly poorly explained that she'd woken up around five that morning with a headache and taken Tylenol, only to discover, as she'd returned the Tylenol to the medicine cabinet, that she'd accidentally taken Tylenol PM, which has soporific qualities, and was as a result "completely out of it."

It was a good story, but I was unable to respond to it with the liveliness it warranted, I told my wife, because I was busy pondering the possibility of my own imminent demise. At that, we left off conversing until we were on our way to the hospital, at which point we undertook reminiscing in a kind of aimless way about elements of our shared past, for instance a certain fellow who attended graduate school in Santa Barbara, California, at the same time as us, and in the same department as my wife, who had many unaccountable personality characteristics. At the time, neither of us could remember his name, although now I remember that his name was Julio, and he was from Puerto Rico. We also talked about another student by the name of Omar who showed up to a seminar class on one occasion wearing a t-shirt advertising the movie *The 40-Year-Old Virgin* and was recriminated at length by the professor (also a native Puerto Rican, coincidentally), who was as appalled by the fact that someone would think to show up to his seminar in a t-shirt with the words *The 40-Year-Old Virgin* printed on it (in all likelihood, he was unfamiliar with the movie to which it referred) as Omar was to find himself being recriminated for his choice of t-shirt, as though what he wore were anyone's business but his own. But then, I think, both my wife and I began to feel that all this looking back on the on the good old times while I was actively pondering the prospect of my own imminent demise was a bit in poor taste, and we fell silent again for the duration of the drive to the hospital. Then we were in the hospital, and then in the surgery waiting room where talking didn't appear to be encouraged unless it was to tell someone, in a hushed tone, something that would cause them to look simultaneously concerned and confused, and then a nurse was calling to me to accompany her to the area where I would be readied for my procedure and the two of us, my wife and I, exchanged a dry kiss, and I followed the nurse through a pair of double doors and down a hallway to a little room, or half-room, enclosed by walls on three sides but only a curtain on the fourth, where I had to take off all my clothes and replace them with a backless hospital gown. The nurse turned her back while I changed, for the sake of privacy, which I found a little beside the point considering the nature of the procedure for which I was now being readied, but in any case that's what she did, and then she turned back around when I told her I was finished and laid me down in the little bed and stuck some little squares to my chest that were then attached to the wires by way of which my vital signs would be monitored during the procedure, and finally she attached an I.V. to a vein in my right wrist, letting it dangle for a moment while she reached for the tube extending from a bag of saline solution to which she subsequently connected it. She taped the tube and I.V. in place, apologized when I said it hurt but did not do anything to relieve the discomfort, and then told me that my nurse would be in shortly, a piece of information that caused me a different sort of pain—the pain of abandonment—since I'd until then been under the impression that this nurse *was* my nurse.

A few minutes later the nurse who truly was my nurse showed up, younger than the first and hale in appearance, sporting a tattoo on her wrist. I tried to establish an affective bond with her, as I thought such a bond would potentially motivate her to work harder to prevent my death than she otherwise might, but she was not receptive to my overtures, and after asking me a couple of questions—my date of birth and address, I guess to make sure I was the person I was supposed to be as opposed to someone trying to scam his way into a free colonoscopy—she went back to a sort of reception area where the nurses who apparently had nothing better to do tended to administrative tasks and engaged in water cooler style conversation. Because she did not close my curtain, and this reception area was directly across from my little half-room, I ended up spending the next several minutes eavesdropping on her conversation with another nurse. The conversation began when my nurse told the other nurse that the next day after work she was planning to go for a run and that the other nurse was free to join her if she liked. The very possibility was quickly ruled out because my nurse wouldn't be finishing work until 4:30 the next day, whereas the other nurse was scheduled to get off at 2:30 and had no interest in hanging around that place an extra two hours. But having established the fundamental impossibility of doing so, the other nurse nonetheless offered a second and consequently superfluous explanation for not wanting to run with my nurse, which was that she wasn't currently running owing to the fact that recently, after running, she'd been getting little pimples around her mouth and eyes. This mention of pimples  led to a very long discussion about how the other nurse, the one who'd been getting pimples after going running, had gone in for a facial at a new skin salon in a nearby town over the weekend. The facial cost three hundred dollars, according to this nurse, a figure my nurse indicated she considered excessive, but then the second nurse brought forth a number of arguments for why spending that much money on a facial was justifiable, including: 1.) That getting a facial that actually worked was, in the long run, less expensive than buying a bunch of products that didn't work, and then, since they didn't work, buying more products that didn't work, and so on *ad infinitum*; 2.) That three hundred dollars was the final price, including tip and sundry expensive products the aesthetician who'd performed her facial assured her would work, as opposed to the expensive products she'd been buying that hadn't worked; 3.) That she'd only tipped on the services and not the products, and 4.) That she'd grown up on a farm and as a result sustained a good deal of sun damage at an early age, especially around her eyes, and the earlier she attended to that damage the better. All in all, these arguments proved convincing to my nurse, who nodded several times as the other nurse elaborated them and when she was finished said, "Well, it *is* your face." At that, the phone rang: it was someone calling my nurse to tell her the time had come to take me back to the procedure room.

From my position of repose on the rolling bed, while she wheeled me down one very long hallway and then another, I mentioned to my nurse that I'd overheard her conversation with the other nurse and was wondering if she knew what the name of the salon where the other nurse had gotten her facial was, as I was myself thinking of getting a facial and it sounded like she'd had a good experience.

"What?" my nurse said. "Oh yeah. She got a facial."

I probably should have left it at that, but I suppose because I was feeling nervous about possibly dying, and feeling nervous was making me feel talkative, as it sometimes does, I mentioned that since the previous summer I'd been breaking out in pimples like I was back in high school or something, and despite the fact that I'd recently read an article on the website for *GQ* magazine about how fashion designers have lately been featuring models with pimples in their runway shows—"The Hottest Thing on the Runway Right Now? Pimples" was the title of it—my pimples still made me feel self-conscious (as they had when I was in high school). As an example, I referred her to the two enormous pimples decorating my forehead; she bent over me, squinted at them for a moment, and said they weren't very noticeable. This lifted my spirits markedly. If I die, I thought, at least people won't look down at my inert body and think to themselves, "And with two enormous pimples, no less."

This bit of elation was cut short by a sudden, unmistakable sensation in my lower abdomen: my bowel, the sensation informed me, indeed was not completely empty. It was, to be sure, an unwelcome discovery, for if the bowel needed to be

completely emptied in order for the
doctor to see what he needed to be
able see, it followed that if the bowel
was not completely empty, the doctor would not be able to see what he
needed to be able see, in which case
I was risking death for nothing and
furthermore would probably have
to do the whole thing all over again.
When I expressed these concerns
to the nurse, she explained that it
wasn't an issue because before get-

ting started the doctor was going to suck out whatever was left
up there with a powerful vacuum cleaner equipped with a flexi-
ble tip suitable for insertion into the anus. This pretty much put
my concerns about ruining the colonoscopy and having to do
another one to bed, but it also got me wondering, aloud, why I'd
gone through a day and a half of fasting and industrial strength
laxatives if in the end they were going to vacuum out my colon
anyway. The nurse didn't offer an explanation, but the fact that
I'd posed the question clearly raised her suspicions, because she
asked me in a very direct tone of voice whether I'd completed
the prep as instructed. I told her I had, although the truth was
that I'd only finished about two-thirds of the second dose, since
at that point taking more just felt like overkill. Next, she asked
me whether my last bowel movements had produced clear yellow liquid. I found this question confusing, since as far as I could
tell liquid could not be both clear and yellow at the same time.

"Clear or yellow?" I asked, hoping to clear things up.

"Clear yellow," she repeated, a bit angrily in my opinion. Then
she turned to wheel me backwards into the procedure room,
where another nurse—a short-haired woman, perhaps fifty-five

or sixty years old and as wide as a barn door, as the saying goes—awaited us.

I was parked in my rolling bed beside the wide, short-haired nurse, who was seated on a squat little stool, and then my nurse went to change the information on a white board hanging near the door, on which the name of another patient and an unfamiliar procedure were listed. She replaced the other patient's name with mine, erased the name of the unfamiliar procedure, and paused. "You're here for an endoscopy or a colonoscopy?" she called over her shoulder. Once that was settled, the wide, short-haired nurse asked me if this was my "welcome to your fifties" colonoscopy? I asked her, by way of reply, "Do I look fifty to you?" and she raised her eyebrows. "Great," I said. "I look like fifty *and* I'm getting pimples like a fucking teenager." I pointed to the blemishes on my forehead. "Those?" the wide, short-haired nurse snorted. "They're hardly even noticeable." I asked her who she was, and she identified herself as a nurse anesthetist and informed me that it was her job to make sure I had a "nice nap."

"So, you're not an actual anesthesiologist?" I asked.

I didn't want to put her on the spot, but at the same time I felt like this was important information considering that when Dr. Patel had originally described the procedure, he'd told me that, in part, it was specifically because an actual anesthesiologist would be in charge of administering the Propofol and monitoring me while I was under its influence that it would not kill me. The answer, in any case, was that she was an actual nurse anesthetist. There was an actual anesthesiologist, as well, but the job of the actual anesthesiologist was to oversee mine and the three other actual anesthetic procedures that were going to be transpiring simultaneously in the same actual hospital, all of them actually administered by actual nurse anesthetists, such as she actually was.

"Don't worry," she added. "I've actually done this a thousand times?"

I noticed a screen to my right and wondered if it was where they'd see the inside of my colon, and the nurse anesthetist told me they would see it in there and in the other screen behind me.

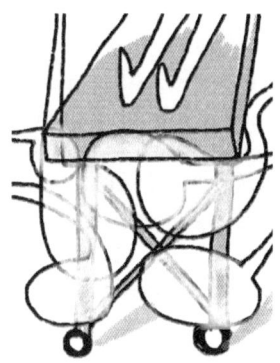

Beside that other screen, a long, black tube, as thick as a garden hose, was looped over a hook. "What's that?" I asked.

"That's what actually goes up your butt," replied the nurse anesthetist.

Presently, the actual anesthesiologist made her appearance. She was young—I don't know if she was younger than I was, but she looked younger than I apparently looked, which is to say, younger than fifty. She introduced herself, informed me that I was going to be receiving Propofol, and then asked me to sign and date a form on a clipboard without giving me time to read it over with care. Then, as she was turning to leave with the clipboard tucked under her arm, she stopped and looked at me with consternation. "I see some bumps on your forehead," she said, touching her own in about the place where my two pimples were situated. "Is that an infection?" I looked at the nurse anesthetist. "I thought you said they weren't noticeable."

She shrugged.

"They're pimples," I told the anesthesiologist.

"Ah," she said with sympathy, and departed.

The nurse anesthetist had undertaken filling a syringe with liquid from a small glass vial; when she finished, she set the empty vial aside and attached the syringe to the I.V. tube running into the vein in my right wrist. I asked her if it was Propofol, she affirmed that it was, and I asked her to hold off on delivering it. "I'd like to talk to the doctor before you put me out," I said. The glance she exchanged with the regular nurse, the one who'd talked with her colleague who'd had the facial and then ignored my inquiries about where that colleague had had her facial, told me that they found this request irksome, but, well, what could be done? To pass the time while we waited, the nurse anesthetist engaged me in some light conversation about my life: what I did for work (I was a professor, I told her, but then amended my answer and identified myself as an instructor, technically speaking, but first and foremost a writer, something I rarely say to strangers in order to avoid that dispiriting conversation wherein they ask me if they've read any of my books and I have to explain that I haven't published any books, although my work has been published in some books) and whether I had any children. When I admitted that I did—one—the anesthetist, as social custom dictates one at that point should, sought further details about him: age (two), personality (linguistic, anxious), and so on. Then she noted that she'd never had any children. "I guess I missed out," she said with indifference. The regular nurse looked over her shoulder and said, "You have a stepdaughter." The nurse anesthetist disagreed. It was true, she conceded, that her partner had a daughter, but that daughter was already an adult by the time she and her partner met, so her relationship to her had never been one that could be characterized as maternal. The regular nurse, who'd in the interim finished whatever she was doing on the other side of the procedure room and was now standing next to my rolling bed, revealed that she had a six-year-old son and a fifteen-year-old stepdaughter. This led to a bit of idle chitchat about things teenagers are into these days, sex and drugs and the usual, and how with her stepdaughter they always tell her that they can make rules for her and give her advice but ultimately, she's responsible for her own decisions. Then I got to talking about how I found the actual birth of my child horrifying, this sudden appearance of a human being where before there had been none, but how now trying to imagine his absence was as impossible as trying to imagine my own.

An uncomfortable silence ensued.

"Where's Dr. Patel," the nurse with the stepchildren said at last. And then, just like that, Dr. Patel was there, striding through the door all dressed in white (a bold move, given the task at hand) with a clipboard of his own tucked under his arm. "Why is he awake?" he asked when he saw me blinking in his direction. The two nurses exchanged another look and then the anesthetist took the lead, recounting how I'd asked to talk to him before she put me under. "Okay," Dr. Patel said. "What do you want to talk about, then?" Needless to say, I hadn't thought that far ahead, so I simply said the first thing that came to mind: "Try not to kill me."

By that time, the nurse with the stepchildren had already rolled me onto my left side, exposing my bare buttocks.

I looked at the anesthetist.

"Pick a dream," she said, and depressed the plunger on the syringe.

As though from a great distance, I heard Dr. Patel say: "Don't worry. As soon as you're out I'll just spit on it and stick it in."

Or perhaps that was just the dream I'd picked.

Wart, Two Ways

I

During our time abroad I am, as at home, diligent about washing my hands; nonetheless, I develop what appears to be a wart on the second knuckle of my right index finger. I go on washing my hands diligently, notwithstanding the fact that, thanks to this wart, I no longer belong to the category of uncontaminated people who must be diligent about washing their hands in the hope of remaining that way, but rather to that of the contaminated people as a result of whose existence uncontaminated people need to be diligent about washing their hands. This begs the question: do the contaminated people as a result of whose existence uncontaminated people need to be diligent about washing their hands also need to be diligent about washing their hands? The answer seems obvious: yes, because that with which any given contaminated person is contaminated is not the same as that with which any other contaminated person may be contaminated, and with which the former might therefore become additionally contaminated.

But I suspect the answer is not as obvious as it seems.

II

During our time abroad I am, as at home, diligent about washing my hands; nonetheless, I develop what appears to be a wart on the second knuckle of my right index finger. At a pharmacy in a subdivision near a series of picturesque coves with beaches that disappear at high tide, a pharmacist wearing a white lab coat who has just finished selling obscenely overpriced shaving cream to the customer in front of me confirms my diagnosis but fails to deduce from it the reason for my visit. When I tell him that I'd like some wart removal ointment, he furrows his brow,[1] points out that the wart is quite small by referring to it using

---

1. In an article published in January of 2018 on *The Daily Beast*, a website of news and commentary, documentary filmmaker Marianne Schaefer Trench describes "hyperactive eyebrows in fiction" as "writers' go-to lazy shorthand for pretty much any emotion," and "imagine[s] a utopia where writers ignore eyebrows altogether and find more original ways to express emotion." I am compensated for this story's necessary exclusion from that utopia by the knowledge that it is not in the nature of utopias to ever actually be achieved

the diminutive form of the noun, and asks me, with apparent skepticism, whether it's bothering me. I tell him that having it is bothering me and he sighs, disappears into the storeroom, and returns holding a small vial sealed with a dropper cap.

"One drop a day for three or four days," he says, passing it to me across the counter, and then pauses before adding, a bit gratuitously from my perspective: "Whatever you do, don't put it on your penis."

Street, Two Ways

The name of the one-way street just down the street from our rented apartment in this city far from home translates, literally, to "John of the Thing," which is strange, but not nearly as strange as the fact that the first street beyond that street, marked one-way in the same direction, is also named "John of the Thing."

In a small city in a faraway country are two streets, side-by-side, each marked one-way in the same direction and each bearing the same strange name: "John of the Thing," or so it translates to English from the local vernacular. This bit of cartographic whimsy strikes the visitor as potentially advantageous, inasmuch as one who has turned onto the wrong street might nevertheless have turned onto the right street, but also potentially disadvantageous, inasmuch as, having turned onto the right street, one might nonetheless turn out to have turned onto the wrong street.

A Shot On the Calle Murguía

Mexico is often portrayed as quite the dangerous place, but during the weeks we'd been in Oaxaca I couldn't have felt safer, which is why I was so surprised to read about the incident, and even more so to read that it had taken place in broad daylight on the Calle Murguía, a lively and heavily-trafficked street I traversed most afternoons on the way to a particularly delicious popsicle stand with my young son either walking beside me or, when his little legs had tired, reclining in his stroller while I pushed him along. What had happened, according to the article published in the newspaper, was that a group of armed men had boarded the bus while it was stopped. It wasn't clear from the article whether it was stopped at a stoplight or stop sign, as a result of backed-up traffic, or because it had pulled up to a marked bus stop, and while from the fact that the door would have had to have been opened in order for the armed men in question to have boarded, it may seem to follow that it was at a bus stop, where the driver usually opens the door as a matter of course, by merely flashing their weapons the men probably could have convinced the driver to open the door in any of the other aforementioned circumstances. Anyhow, upon boarding the bus the armed men—one of them, I would assume, although in the article the verb was conjugated in the third person plural—knocked the driver unconscious with the butt end of a firearm and, the driver now slumped over his oversized steering wheel (this detail was not included in the newspaper, but when I think of bus drivers I always think of those big, oversized steering wheels they have to grapple with), the group of men gathered around an otherwise unremarkable looking young fellow, a teenager, seated in the back row of the bus, and, thus surrounding him in a semicircle with their weapons drawn, ordered all of the other passengers off the bus. Once the bus was empty but for the band of armed men, the teenager, and the unconscious bus driver, the teenager was asked whether he was the one known as "El Halcón"—the Falcon. He responded in the affirmative and without further ado the men opened fire, riddling his body with bullets. Now, the one known as "El Halcón" was dead and, having evidently accomplished their mission, the killers quickly disembarked and dispersed, well before the police (assault rifles strapped across their backs as useless as minstrels' guitars, no doubt) arrived on the scene. Per my rudimentary and probably incorrect understanding of how these things generally worked in Mexico, I conjectured that agreements had been forged ahead of time between the armed men and the police such that, whether in exchange for a small cash payout or merely to avoid the inconvenience of becoming targets themselves, the latter had taken care to steer clear of the area during the carrying out of the murder, and for a few minutes thereafter—but not so long as to make their intentions (or lack of the same) impossibly obvious.

I thought, h*ow could this happen on the Calle Murguía?*, and then I remembered what a Colombian acquaintance had recently said to me when I observed how friendly everyone in Oaxaca was: "Amables hasta que te maten," meaning, "Friendly until they kill you." Then I reread the article and discovered, on this second reading, that the incident in question had in fact taken place on the Calle Murguía in the center of another city in the state of Oaxaca, and not, as I'd originally thought, in the capital city itself, where I'd been staying. This discovery effectively did away with the cognitive dissonance (not quite resolved by recalling that Mexicans, like everyone else in the world, cease to seem friendly when they are killing you) produced by news of a murder in cold blood on the Calle Murguía with which I was personally familiar, but in so doing must have opened up the necessary mental space for a couple of questions that had not crossed my mind the first time through to make their way to the surface. First was the question of from precisely whom the author of the newspaper article had gathered all of the details included in his description of the incident if everyone had been ordered off the bus except the victim, who was dead, and could therefore tell no tales, and the driver, who had been knocked unconscious. Here, it was not difficult to hypothesize an answer. For example, couldn't the driver have recovered from his stupor but for obvious reasons chosen to go on feigning unconsciousness, and therefore, with his head still slumped over the oversized steering wheel but his senses wide awake, heard everything that happened and later given his "earwitness" account to the journalist? Another possibility—perhaps more likely, considering the risks giving such an account might have posed to the driver's own safety—was that the criminals themselves had divulged the details of the killing to the author of the article, if only to ensure that it was thoroughly reported: having a bad reputation, after all, is probably your most important job if you work in the enforcement sector of the underground economy, and disseminating that bad reputation as important a part of that job as actually earning it. The other question that arose during my second pass through the article—specifically, the question of why the one known as "El Halcón," when asked by the men pointing their weapons at him whether or not he was the one known as "El Halcón," responded in the affirmative—was more vexing. No, it probably would not have made a difference if he'd lied and said, "I think that was the guy sitting next to me," or, "You've got it all wrong, I'm the one they call the *Eagle*," because yes, the men pointing their weapons at him probably already knew the answer to this question that was, therefore, probably posed only rhetorically—and yet, considering the circumstances in which the one who was, indeed, known as "El Halcón" found himself at the time, it seemed to me then, as it still does now, that he might as well have given it a shot.

On the Kindness of Others

On the other side of a bridge in need of repair I drive past a peculiar gentleman. On the back of his bright yellow jacket the words "Volunteers <u>ARE</u> Superheroes"—just so, with the "are" underlined and in all capital letters—have been written in black paint, and with a pair of gloved hands he holds aloft a cardboard sign on which he, or for all I know someone else, has written, with probably the same black paint, "Thank You, Volunteers!" A couple of days earlier, and at a different time of the day, I saw the same gentleman walking along the edge of a busy highway, wearing the same jacket and holding the same sign; it is very cold out, but he must be spending a lot of time doing this, and covering a lot of ground. Now, I glance in my rearview mirror and although there is not another car in sight, he is still holding the sign as high above his head as the length of his arms permits.

By chance, I am on my way to a café I often go to in order to write, a daily labor the performance of which provides me with that regular experience of challenge and subsequent accomplishment that is, according to recent research, crucial to the attainment of personal happiness. As I have never earned a taxable quantity of income from this labor, I ask myself, *might the time I spend writing not be considered a form of volunteerism?* I would very much like for this to be the case, in particular because the same recent research indicates that altruistic activity also contributes to the attainment of personal happiness. But there exists a certain presumption that volunteer work, in order to be considered as such, must be of some kind of service to someone other than the person performing it, and I am forced to admit that in this regard my work as a writer likely falls short.

It occurs to me that much the same could be said of this peculiar gentleman's no doubt equally unremunerated work walking the local highways and byways with his painted sign and yellow jacket were it not for the fact that, in so doing, he has given me something to write about, in so doing making a valuable contribution to my attainment of personal happiness.

Too Much Too Soon

In the fall I bought a new pair of running shoes that made me feel five pounds lighter when I put them on, and with the assistance of these new running shoes I began increasing my daily mileage and pace, with excellent results. This carried on until, in or about late December or early January, I injured my groin. At first, I thought it was just an ache or pain, not unlike the other various aches or pains I typically experienced after my runs, but instead of abating with a few days rest this ache or pain lingered, and then began to get worse and worse; at last, I realized it was not an ache or pain at all, but a genuine injury. Months have passed since then (now it is spring), during which time I have tried my best to cure this groin injury on my own using a combination of internet research and proverbial commonsense. For instance, I reduced the frequency, pace, and duration of my runs; then, I acquired a lacrosse ball, per the advice of an online video about groin injuries, and in the mornings and evenings began spending a period of time with it nuzzled into the part of my groin where the injury is located, rolling back and forth on top of it in a vaguely perverse manner.

The injury is located, speaking of where the injury is located, in my uppermost and innermost adductor muscle, all the way up there in the crease where right leg and crotch come together. It is hardly lost on me that this means that while I am happy and even eager to discuss it with pretty much anyone at all—my supposed friends, the people who work at the café where I go some mornings to write, the people who work at the café where I go other mornings to write, the students in the classes I teach in exchange for the money I spend on things like coffee (for writing) and running shoes (for injuring my groin), and so on—if it were located just a half-inch or so to the left, it would be not an injury to my groin but to my testicle, which I would be willing to discuss with a much smaller selection of people, and that if it were located just a half inch further left than that, it would be not an injury to my testicle but to my penis, in which case I probably wouldn't discuss it with anyone except my wife, and even then only because, in the best of worlds, she would be bound to discover it for herself sooner or later.

But maybe that's not quite true, either. For instance, many years ago, nearly twenty, when I was young and living in Los

Angeles with barely enough money to pay for coffee at the café
I went to in the evenings to read (I wrote in my apartment
at a desk I'd stolen, not quite accidentally but not exactly on
purpose, either, from the surplus furniture lot at a nearby university) and was carrying on, with a young acting student who
worked many evenings at that same café, a sexual relationship
distinguished above all my difficulty achieving and sustaining an erection, I thought I'd discovered the mark of venereal
disease on my penis, a little angry-looking red bump, and
rushed without even calling to make an appointment to the
industrially proportioned medical center to which the community college at which I was working as a part-time instructor
subsidized my access. A couple of hours later I was shut inside
an office with Juanita Graham, the nurse practitioner to whom
I'd been assigned when I enrolled there as a patient, sharing
with her a good deal more information about the condition of
and recent activities engaged in by my penis than I suspect she
cared to know, and I did not hesitate for even a moment when
she interrupted my monologue with an order to "drop your
pants." Using a pair of gloved hands, she examined the exposed
penis, turning it this way and that like someone trying to determine whether a fish that has been sitting a few days too long
in the refrigerator is still suitable for cooking, before finally
(I say "finally" because the time spent waiting for a report on
the wellbeing of your penis feels long even if it is, according to
the clock, quite brief) declaring it a case of folliculitis: not a
venereal disease, in other words, but an ingrown hair. "Black
men frequently get them on their beards," she explained, a bit
incongruously I thought. Then I pulled my pants up, she wrote
me a prescription for a treatment cream, I had the prescription filled at the medical center's in-house pharmacy (an efficient business model), I applied the cream to the ingrown hair

once or twice a day for a certain period of time the duration of which I could not possibly recall from my present vantage-point, and soon the little angry looking red bump was looking not quite so red and angry, and not too long after that it was gone altogether and life went back to normal, which was, at the time, not actually very normal.

I've had few sexual partners in my life (to put it otherwise, I've had fewer sexual partners than most of the sexual partners I've had had had by the time we partnered sexually), so the fact that Juanita Graham handled my penis makes her a member of a very small club. What distinguishes her from its other members, of course, is first and foremost that her handling of my penis was not sexual in nature, neither on her end nor mine, but also, and perhaps more importantly, that as far as I know she is the only one among them who, presuming the Juanita Graham described in the obituary I find online as having lived most of her adult life in Los Angeles where she worked as a nurse practitioner at the medical center at which I was a patient during the time period in question is the same Juanita Graham who once compared my penis to black man's beard, is no longer among the living. According to the obituary, which otherwise makes no mention of her cause of death, "[Juanita] said many times that when she passed away, she hoped it was while playing tennis. Her wish came true, but for those who loved her, far too soon."

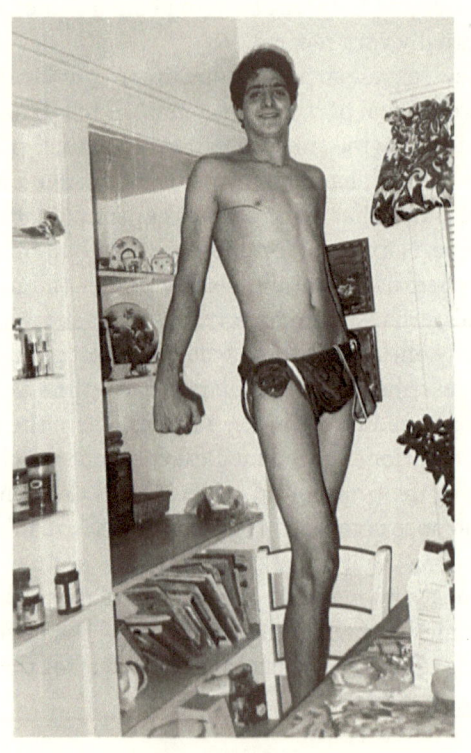

The author circa 1994

About the author

Eli S. Evans was born in Milwaukee, Wisconsin, back when the city motto was "A Great Place on a Great Lake."

Is Milwaukee still a great place? Is the lake still merely Great, or has it become superior? Our readers may want to know, but we relay Eli's biography exactly as he shared it with us.

About the cat

The miscellaneous cat illustrations sprinkled throughout the text depict Chizu, illustrator Patrick Giroux's pandemic muse and general benefactor.

A note on the type

This book is set in Cardea, a typeface designed by David Cabianca in his spare time between writing treatises on the sublime uselessness of graphic design and teaching architectural theory. It is a muscular typeface, reminiscent of the early work of body-sculptor Charles Atlas or the author circa 1994. It is a typeface that glistens and gleams on the page.

*Other publications available from the
Moon Rabbit Books & Ephemera Corporation*

Johnny America #9

Which consists of thirty-six pages of very short shorts, illustrations, and a comic strip which confuses and delights us. As with previous issues, it sports a silkscreen cover, hand-stitched thread binding, and smells vaguely of citrus. $5

Johnny America #10

Forthcoming in the Fall of 2021. This will be our newest, best, and the most erotic collection of fiction, humor, and other miscellany yet produced from the ten-hundred block of New Jersey Street in Lawrence, Kansas. $5

You Gotta Play to Win

Forthcoming in the Spring of 2021. A one-off 'zine of Mark Brown's collected reviews of lottery tickets. Because why not? Risograph cover. $3

www.moonrabbitbooks.com

www.ingramcontent.com/pod-product-compliance
Lightning Source LLC
Chambersburg PA
CBHW021133080526
44587CB00012B/1260